Also by Steve Langford:

Why the Bible Is So Hard to Understand …
and Tips to Understanding It

A God-Shaped World: Exploring Jesus's Teachings about the
Kingdom of God and the Implications for the Church Today

The Fruit of the Spirit

The Path That Leads to Loving as Jesus Loved

Steve Langford

WESTBOW
PRESS®
A DIVISION OF THOMAS NELSON
& ZONDERVAN

Unless otherwise indicated, all scripture quotations are from New Revised Standard Version Bible, copyright © 1989 National Council of the Churches of Christ in the United States of America. Used by permission. All rights reserved worldwide.

Scripture quotations marked (NIV) are taken from the Holy Bible, New International Version®, NIV®. Copyright © 1973, 1978, 1984, 2011 by Biblica, Inc.™ Used by permission of Zondervan. All rights reserved worldwide. www. zondervan.com The "NIV" and "New International Version" are trademarks registered in the United States Patent and Trademark Office by Biblica, Inc.™

This book is a work of non-fiction. Unless otherwise noted, the author and the publisher make no explicit guarantees as to the accuracy of the information contained in this book and in some cases, names of people and places have been altered to protect their privacy.

WestBow Press books may be ordered through booksellers or by contacting:

WestBow Press
A Division of Thomas Nelson & Zondervan
1663 Liberty Drive
Bloomington, IN 47403
www.westbowpress.com
1 (866) 928-1240

Because of the dynamic nature of the Internet, any web addresses or links contained in this book may have changed since publication and may no longer be valid. The views expressed in this work are solely those of the author and do not necessarily reflect the views of the publisher, and the publisher hereby disclaims any responsibility for them.

Any people depicted in stock imagery provided by Getty Images are models, and such images are being used for illustrative purposes only. Certain stock imagery © Getty Images.

ISBN: 978-1-9736-5294-6 (sc)
ISBN: 978-1-9736-5293-9 (hc)
ISBN: 978-1-9736-5295-3 (e)

Library of Congress Control Number: 2019901458

Print information available on the last page.

WestBow Press rev. date: 2/20/2019

Contents

To Etta, who has shared the journey with
me and loved me as Jesus loved

PREFACE

The distinguishing mark of the life and ministry of Jesus was love: self-giving, servant love.[1] Jesus also identified such love as the identifying mark of his followers (John 13:34–35). The apostle Paul echoed the teachings of Jesus. Paul also identified Jesus's love as the distinguishing mark of the follower of Jesus.

In his letter to the Galatians, Paul identified love as the number one characteristic of the fruit of the Spirit (Galatians 5:22–23). In his letter to the Corinthian church, he identified love as the indispensable element of living as a follower of Jesus (1 Corinthians 13). Reason would suggest, then, that such love would be the distinguishing characteristic of the followers of Jesus today as well as the distinguishing characteristic of churches, the communities of Christ's followers.

In the fruit of the Spirit, Paul not only identified love as the number one characteristic of a follower of Jesus, he also explained *how* such love is possible in the life of every follower of Jesus. Love can be the defining mark of the follower of Jesus through the empowering work of the Spirit. This book is an exploration of the fruit of the Spirit that Paul identified:

love, joy, peace, patience, kindness, generosity, faithfulness, gentleness, and self-control. It probes the interrelated nature of the nine traits Paul identified and how they work together to enable the follower of Jesus to love as Jesus loved.

This book is offered with the prayer that the followers of Jesus today will be known by their self-giving, servant love. The fruit of the Spirit is the secret to doing so.

GALATIANS 5:13–26[2]

For you were called to freedom, brothers and sisters; only do not use your freedom as an opportunity for self-indulgence, but through love become slaves to one another.

For the whole law is summed up in a single commandment, "You shall love your neighbor as yourself."

If, however, you bite and devour one another, take care that you are not consumed by one another.

Live by the Spirit, I say, and do not gratify the desires of the flesh.

For what the flesh desires is opposed to the Spirit, and what the Spirit desires is opposed to the flesh; for these are opposed to each other, to prevent you from doing what you want.

But if you are led by the Spirit, you are not subject to the law.

Now *the works of the flesh* are obvious: fornication, impurity, licentiousness, idolatry, sorcery, enmities, strife, jealousy, anger, quarrels, dissensions, factions, envy, drunkenness, carousing, and things like these. I am warning you, as I warned you before: those who do such things will not inherit the kingdom of God.

By contrast, the fruit of the Spirit is love, joy, peace, patience, kindness, generosity, faithfulness, gentleness, and self-control. There is no law against such things.

And those who belong to Christ Jesus have crucified the flesh with its passions and desires.

If we live by the Spirit, *let us also be guided by the Spirit.*

Let us not become conceited, competing against one another, envying one another.

Chapter 1

The Fruit of the Spirit versus the Works of the Flesh

Paul's identification of the fruit of the Spirit is the central part of a larger teaching. The path that leads to loving as Jesus loved cuts through the landscape of this larger passage. Thus, this larger context guides our understanding of the fruit of the Spirit.

The Flesh and the Works of the Flesh

The nine traits Paul identified as the fruit of the Spirit stand in marked contrast to what Paul called *the flesh*. Paul emphasized this contrast with the words with which he introduced the fruit of the Spirit: "by contrast." This contrast gives us clues for understanding Paul's thinking in the fruit of the Spirit.

Paul had a deep understanding of human nature. His use of the term *the flesh* referred to more than the physical desires of the body. It was the shorthand term he used to speak of the self-focused, self-serving spirit that is inherent to our human condition. *The flesh* refers to our default nature. In today's language, *the flesh* refers to the ego-centric needs and desires that drive how we live and govern how we relate to others.

These ego needs lead us to unconsciously operate out of a what's-in-it-for-me spirit. This self-focused, self-serving spirit is driven by deep-seated anxiety and fear, robbing us of joy and peace. Living out of this default nature, we live out of a spirit of scarcity. We think in terms of "us and them" and "me and mine." We easily become impatient with others and are critical and judgmental of them. We distance ourselves— emotionally and physically—from "the other." We use our power and abilities to take care of me and mine, often using those abilities against "the other." This default nature stands in marked contrast to the self-giving love that the Spirit seeks to produce within the followers of Jesus.

> The *flesh* was the shorthand term Paul used to speak of the self-focused, self-serving spirit that is inherent to our human condition. It refers to our default nature

Paul spoke of the impact on human relationships of this self-serving, what's-in-it-for-me spirit as *the works of the flesh.*[3]

> Now, the works of the flesh are obvious: fornication, impurity, licentiousness, idolatry, sorcery, enmities, strife, jealousy, anger, quarrels, dissensions, factions, envy,

drunkenness, carousing, and things like these
(Galatians 5:19–21).

This listing divides into three broad categories of behavior
that the self-serving, what's-in-it-for-me spirit produces. The
first set of behaviors involves the self-indulgence of physical
appetites and desires in the relentless pursuit of pleasure:
fornication, impurity, licentiousness, drunkenness, and
carousing. These behaviors reflect an insatiable hunger for
"more." They seek to fill an inner emotional-psychological-
spiritual emptiness through the gratification of physical
desires.

The second group of behaviors expresses a desire for
power. Idolatry and sorcery were attempts to have power
over the unnamed forces beyond the physical realm. These
practices sought to manipulate those powers for one's own
profit and advantage. They reflect a desire for control.

Finally, the flesh produces division and broken
relationships: enmities, strife, jealousy, anger, quarrels,
dissensions, factions, and envy. In this listing of the works
of the flesh, Paul tied the brokenness and chaos of human
relationships directly to the self-serving, what's-in-it-for-me
spirit that is our default human nature: *the flesh.*

The Law: The Human Attempt
to Control the Flesh

The way humans have historically dealt with such life-
depleting behaviors is through laws. We create religious,

moral, and legal codes that define what is acceptable and what is not. These laws become tools we use in seeking to control our basic nature and the chaos it creates. This reliance upon law is the larger context of Paul's fruit of the Spirit. In his letter to the churches of Galatia, Paul warned his readers about the inadequacy of the law, first, as a means of relating to God and, then, as a means of living as the followers of Jesus.[4]

First, he reminded the Galatians that grace was the basis of relationship with God—not obedience to the law. His letter challenged the teachings of those teachers who had come into the churches of Galatia behind Paul. Whereas Paul had proclaimed that God relates to us out of grace, these teachers insisted that the Gentiles had to be circumcised and submit to the Jewish Law.

Paul's letter is full of anger and disappointment as he confronted this emphasis upon law. He challenged his readers' thinking with hard statements and pointed questions.[5] Paul appealed to the example of Abraham to argue that faith, not obedience to the Law, is the basis of our relationship with God (Galatians 3:6–9). He argued that those who attempted to relate to God based upon obedience to the Law must obey all of the Law without fail and, thus, are under a curse (Galatians 3:10–14; 5:3). Paul called the Law a guardian or disciplinarian designed to lead us to God's grace. The violation of the Law creates an awareness of sin (Galatians 3:19–26) and, therein, the awareness of the need of grace.

In chapter 5 of his letter, Paul advanced his argument. Having reaffirmed grace as the basis of the Galatians' relationship with God, he turned to what was to guide how they lived. Paul argued that the followers of Jesus do not live by obeying the Law because they have been set free from the Law. "For freedom Christ has set us free. Stand firm, therefore,

> **The Law can tell us what to do, but it cannot empower us to do what it says**

and do not submit again to a yoke of slavery" (Galatians 5:1). Here, Paul spoke of living by the Law as living in slavery, under a harsh taskmaster. Instead of living by the Law, the followers of Christ live by the Spirit. They are guided and empowered by the Spirit.

Paul also addressed the issue of the Law in his letter to the churches in Rome. In that letter, Paul described the Law as powerless. It can tell us what to do, but it cannot empower us to do what it says.

The Spirit, by contrast, does what the Law cannot do. The Spirit empowers us to live the ways of God[6] by setting us free from the power of the flesh. The Spirit produces the fruit of the Spirit within us. In his description of the fruit of the Spirit, Paul noted: "There is no law against such things" (Galatians 5:23).

Live by the Spirit: Moving beyond the Patterns of the Flesh

The Spirit, not the Law, is how the followers of Jesus deal with the flesh and the chaos it produces in human relationships.

> Live by the Spirit, I say, and do not gratify the desires of the flesh. For what the flesh desires is opposed to the Spirit, and what the Spirit desires is opposed to the flesh; for these are opposed to each other. (Galatians 5:16–17).

The Spirit moves us beyond the patterns associated with the flesh. To live by the Spirit is to live in an intentional, conscious relationship with God, allowing the Spirit, rather than the Law, to be our guide for living. The Spirit teaches us the ways of God that Jesus taught and then guides us in how to put those ways into practice in our relationships.[7]

To live by the Spirit also involves depending upon the Spirit for the power to do what we cannot do in our own strength. The things Jesus taught go against the natural inclinations of our default human nature. Thus, we need a power beyond our own to live as his followers. So, to live by the Spirit is to live in glad dependency on the Spirit for guidance and power. The Spirit becomes our silent partner who enables us to learn and live the ways of God that Jesus taught.

In this section of his letter (Galatians 5:16–26), Paul identified two things the Spirit produces in our lives. The Spirit leads us beyond "the flesh," our default, fear-based, self-focused, self-serving, what's-in-it-for-me spirit. This work of the Spirit is more than controlling the works of the flesh. The Spirit moves us beyond the old reactive patterns that produce the works of the flesh. But the Spirit's work is not complete until a new spirit replaces our old default spirit, until new ways of relating replace our old fear-based patterns. The Spirit's work is not complete until our lives are filled with the fruit of the Spirit. The Spirit empowers us to love as Jesus loved.

For the whole law is summed up in a single commandment, "You shall love your neighbor as yourself," Galatians 5:14

CHAPTER 2

The Path to Loving as Jesus Loved

The nine traits that Paul identified as the fruit of the Spirit are not nine separate, independent abilities. Rather, they are interrelated and interdependent. No single trait stands alone. That's why Paul spoke of them as the fruit (singular) of the Spirit rather than the fruits (plural) of the Spirit. The fruit (singular) of the Spirit stands in contrast to the works (plural) of the flesh.

These nine traits are the same traits we find in the life of Jesus. Thus, they show us what Christlike spirituality looks like. In producing these traits in us, the Spirit is working to make us like Christ and empowering us to love as Jesus loved. These traits are the indicators of the Spirit's work in us, leading us into spiritual maturity.

The fruit of the Spirit is not a level of maturity we attain once and for all. It can become the perspective from which we live as we grow spiritually, but this Spirit-empowered way of relating must be chosen over and over again. The fruit of the Spirit is how the Spirit empowers us to relate *in the midst of* any given relationship, in any situation, at any given time.

The nine traits identified as the fruit of the Spirit fall into three categories that correspond to the three categories of the works of the flesh identified in chapter 1. The ability to love as Jesus loved is the *goal* of the Spirit's work. Self-giving, servant love is rooted in and flows out of joy and peace. These first three traits describe the spirit the Spirit fosters within us. As long as we live with anxiety, fear, and anger, our ability to love will be thwarted. This spirit of love, joy, and peace stands in contrast to the self-indulgent spirit that is a part of the works of the flesh.

The next five traits are all relational terms. They describe what love looks like in human relationships. Moving beyond anxiety, fear, and anger into a spirit of love, joy, and peace sets us free to relate to others with patience, kindness, generosity, faithfulness, and gentleness. Grace and forgiveness shape the way we live in relationship. This grace-based way of relating is diametrically opposed to the alienation and broken relationships that are a part of the works of the flesh.

The final trait is the key trait that makes the other eight traits possible: self-control. The Spirit teaches us to recognize and manage the anxiety and fear that drive our emotional reactivity. Managing our anxiety and fear positions us to experience the joy and peace the Spirit gives. Living out of joy and peace, the Spirit-empowered follower of Jesus is in a position to choose to live out of patience, kindness, generosity, faithfulness, and gentleness. In other words, the Spirit empowers the follower of Jesus to love *in that particular moment, situation, and relationship.* This spirit of self-control is diametrically opposed to the grasping for power and control (idolatry, sorcery) that is a part of the works of the flesh.

The Spirit sets us free from the power of our self-serving, what's-in-it-for-me spirit, empowering us to love as Jesus loved.

The Path to Loving as Jesus Loved

Love
The Goal of the Spirit's Work

Joy and Peace
The Spirit out of Which Love Flows

Patience, Kindness, Generosity, Faithfulness, Gentleness
What Love Looks Like
in Relationships

Self-control
The Key to Loving as Jesus Loved

CHAPTER 3

Love, Joy, and Peace: The Spirit with Which We Live

The first three traits Paul listed as the fruit of the Spirit reflect the spirit out of which the follower of Jesus lives. Love, joy, and peace are aspects of the interior realm. They speak of the attitude and disposition of the heart.

These three interrelated traits remind us that the interior realm is the primary realm of the Spirit's work. The Spirit is at work to transform our hearts and minds. The evidence of that transformation is seen in the spirit out of which we live.

Our relationships flow out of and reflect the inner spirit of our lives.

That spirit governs how we view and treat others. Herein is a foundational truth underlying the fruit of the Spirit: our relationships flow out of and reflect the inner spirit of our lives.

The spirit or inner disposition of our lives is foundational to being able to love. It governs how we respond (as opposed to reacting) to life's events as well as how we relate to others in the midst of those events. The Spirit produces within us a spirit of joy and peace that enables us to love.

Because we were created in the image of God,[8] we were created with the capacity to live out of love, joy, and peace. God's very nature is self-giving, servant love.[9] We were created to share God's nature and participate in God's life. In other words, we were created for love, joy, and peace. But life's experiences conditioned us to live out of a different spirit. The formative events in our lives trained us to live out of anxiety and fear rather than peace and out of anger and negativity rather than joy. This anxiety and fear, anger and negativity grow out of perceived threats to our basic ego needs. As we saw in chapter 1, this anxiety-shaped spirit is self-seeking and self-serving (Paul's term, *the flesh*) as opposed to the spirit of love for which we were created. This fear-based spirit that was created by life's experiences is our default nature. We automatically react out of this self-serving spirit. It lies beyond our conscious awareness until we learn to recognize and manage it through the power of the Spirit (self-control).

Like all of the nine traits, these first three traits are interdependent. One leads to the other. The apex is self-giving, servant love, but the ability to love flows out of the other two. Being at peace enables us to experience joy. Peace and joy free us to love.

The spirit or inner disposition of our lives is foundational to being able to love

---

CHAPTER 4

The Fruit of the Spirit Is Love

The first of the nine traits identified as the fruit of the Spirit is love. Love is the premier trait. As in the life of Jesus, love is the distinguishing mark of the follower of Jesus.[10] The *goal* of the Spirit's work in our lives is to enable us to love as Jesus loved. The other eight Spirit-produced traits are the path that leads us to love. They identify the *spirit* out of which love flows while telling us *what* love looks like and *how* we can love as Jesus loved.

The Nature of Love

The word Paul used for love is the word commonly used in the New Testament to speak of God's kind of love: *agape*. This love does not refer to what one feels about another, although how we feel about another will change when we relate to the other out of love. Agape refers to how we choose to live in relationship with another person. It is about how we view and treat the other. Thus, love is more about *the will* than it is about emotions or feelings.

Two texts from the writings of John point to the nature of God's kind of love. In John 13:34, Jesus gave his disciples a new commandment: "I give you a new commandment, that you love one another. Just as I have loved you, you also should love one another." That commandment is repeated in John 15:12: "This is my commandment, that you love one another as I have loved you." The next verse, John 15:13, describes what it means to love as Jesus loved: "No one has greater love than this, to lay down one's life for one's friends."

The love Jesus described focuses on the other and seeks the good, the growth, and the well-being of the other. The means by which the other's good is sought is the giving of oneself—to lay down one's life. To love as Jesus loved is to give of who I am and what I have for the good of another. That self-giving involves the giving of all that God has entrusted to me: my time, my energies, my abilities, my knowledge, my experiences, my financial resources, and my material possessions.

A second text from the writings of John echoes Jesus's understanding of love. 1 John 4:8 identifies love as the central characteristic of God's character: "God is love." Verses 9 and 10 then describe the nature of God's love:

> God's love was revealed among us in this way: God sent his only Son into the world so that we might live through him. In this is love, not that we loved God but that God loved us and

sent his Son to be the atoning sacrifice for our
sins.

This text teaches us that God's love is other-centered, focused
on the other. It is expressed in actions that address the other's
need and seeks the other's wholeness. In other words, God's
love is life-giving. These actions involve self-sacrifice as God
gives the Son for our good. Such love is given freely, as a gift.
It is not tied to what we deserve. Thus, it takes the initiative
in the relationship.

God's kind of love is the expression of a servant spirit.
It gives freely of self, often at great sacrifice. It uses power
on behalf of the other, actively seeking their well-being
and wholeness. It is uplifting, empowering, and life-giving.
This kind of love is the opposite of our default nature. It
transcends the ego's needs and the self-focused, self-serving,
what's-in-it-for-me spirit that is rooted in those needs.

But before we move on, another word is needed about this
love. Jesus's parable in Matthew 25:31–46 reminds us that
our love as Jesus's followers is not limited to "one another"
and "one's friends." It is not limited to "me and mine." It
also includes "the least of these" that Jesus identified: the
hungry, the thirsty, the stranger, the naked, the sick, and
those in prison. In other words, to love as Jesus loved is to
serve those with the least resources: the poor, the powerless,
the vulnerable.[11] God's kind of love does not discriminate.
It does not pick and choose who to love or who deserves to
receive love. Love sees each person through the eyes of God
and, thereby, responds to each as a beloved child of God.

The parable also reminds us that God's kind of love is a get-involved, get-your-hands-dirty, make-a-difference kind of love. It is risk-taking, forget-about-playing-it-safe kind of love. It is who-cares-what-people-think kind of love. It is a self-giving love that intentionally gets involved in the lives of others so that they might experience the life God desires for them.

The Spirit is at work within each of us to empower us to love with God's kind of love. The Spirit is creating the heart of a servant within each of us so that we can love as Jesus loved.

> **The Spirit is creating the heart of a servant within each of us so that we can love as Jesus loved.**

Relationships: The Arena of Love

The writings of the John emphasize the self-giving, servant nature of God's kind of love. Paul's writings describe what God's kind of love looks like in specific terms. In two different letters, Paul describes what love is: in the fruit of the Spirit (Galatians 5:22–23) and 1 Corinthians 13. In both descriptions, Paul described what love looks like in relationships. In the fruit of the Spirit, Paul described what love is. In 1 Corinthians 13, he described what love is not. Paul's descriptions remind us that the only way we can love is by intentionally and consciously living in relationship with another. Relationships are the arena in which we love.

Five of the traits Paul identified in the fruit of the Spirit are relational terms. They describe what it looks like to love another. Patience, kindness, generosity, faithfulness, and gentleness describe how we relate to another when we live out of self-giving, servant love. These terms draw a picture of what it looks like to relate to another person out of grace. We will explore grace-based relationships more fully in chapter 6. Here, I'll present a brief sketch.

The Spirit empowers us to relate to others out of grace and, thereby, to love as Jesus loved. The Spirit empowers us to be patient, kind, generous, faithful, and gentle as we relate to the other person. Love is *patient*. When we love as Jesus loved, we no longer judge others by how they measure up to our standards and expectations. We accept them where they are, as they are, patiently dealing with the weaknesses and failings that are a normal part of being human.

Love is *kind*. Kindness and gentleness are companions. They speak of how we treat the other person. When we love as Jesus loved, we are no longer critical, judgmental, and condemning of others when they don't measure up to our standards and expectations. We refuse to function out of merit-based thinking. Instead, we are kind to them, choosing to practice generosity.

Love always includes *generosity*. When we love as Jesus loved, we give generously and freely to the other. We are generous with our understanding, with our compassion, with our patience, and with our forgiveness. Such generosity is what enables us to be kind. In addition, we give generously and freely of ourselves: our time, our energies, our abilities, our knowledge, and our experiences. Of course, our generosity also includes all the material wealth that God has entrusted to us.

Love is *faithful*. When we live out of love, we refuse to give up on the other person or abandon the relationship. We keep on keeping on—even when the relationship becomes difficult or painful.

Love is *gentle*. Gentleness speaks of our touch on the other's life and of how we use our power in relation to them. When we love as Jesus loved, we touch others in ways that are healing and helpful. We are conscious of not touching them—with our voices, with our hands, with our attitudes, and with our looks—in ways that hurt and wound.

In these five traits, Paul described how the Spirit empowers us to relate to others. He, in effect, described *what love is*. In his description of love in 1 Corinthians 13, he emphasized *what love is not*.

> Love is patient; love is kind; love is not envious or boastful or arrogant or rude. It does not insist on its own way; it is not irritable or resentful; it does not rejoice in wrongdoing, but rejoices in the truth. It bears all things, believes all things, hopes all things, endures all things. (1 Corinthians 13:4–7)

Paul began his description with two of the traits he identified in the fruit of the Spirit: patient and kind. Paul then moved into a series of phrases that describe what love is not. He then identified what love does. Paul's description of what love is not divides into two groupings: how we treat the other and what is in our hearts.

In relating to another, Paul said love is *not rude*. To be rude is to treat another person with disrespect with our words, our actions, our attitudes, or our looks. When we love as Jesus loved, we treat the other with dignity and respect—as a beloved child of God. Love is *not irritable*. When we love as Jesus loved, we are not easily angered by what the other says or does. We are patient, putting up with those things that might otherwise stir frustration and anger within us. Love is *not resentful*. Resentment is anger that we hold onto. When we love as Jesus loved, we do not keep score of how the other wronged or hurt us. We do not carry grudges. We forgive.

Paul's description of what love is not included those things in us that block our ability to love. As long as we carry these things in our hearts, we cannot love. Paul says that love moves us beyond these limiting attitudes. Love is *not jealous*. Jealousy is more than wanting what another has. Jealousy is a competitive spirit that doesn't want the other to have what they have. It is a competitive spirit that wants to be in a one-up position with the other. This spirit wants to be better than the other. Jealousy is anger that what the other has puts them in a one-up position in relation to us. A jealous spirit blocks our ability to love.

Love is *not boastful*. Boasting or bragging is more than saying how good or intelligent or important I am. It is a way of saying, "I am better than you." Boasting expresses an arrogant spirit. A boastful spirit blocks our ability to love.

Love is *not arrogant.* Arrogance is the attitude of being better than others. It is expressed in treating others as though they are less than. Arrogance blocks our ability to love.

Love *does not insist on its own way.* Being demanding or controlling or willful or domineering is a subtle form of arrogance. It is saying, through my words and actions, that "my way is best." A controlling, willful spirit cannot love.

Each of these things that Paul said love is not reflects a competitive spirit. They are rooted in thinking of the other in terms of *better than and less than.* In the first group of statements (rude, irritable, and resentful), Paul said love does not treat the other as though they were less than. In the second set of statements, Paul said that love does not act as though I am better than the other. Love moves us beyond the competitive spirit with its *better than* and *less than* thinking.

Love moves us beyond *better than-less than* thinking

Love enables us to see each person as a beloved child of God. It seeks what is good for the other. It seeks that which is life-giving for everyone. Both of Paul's descriptions of love remind us that love is about relationships. It is about how we view and treat others. The Spirit is at work to empower us to be patient, kind, generous, faithful, and gentle in how we relate to others. The Spirit is moving us beyond those attitudes and behaviors rooted in our fear-based, self-serving, competitive nature that block our ability to love.

The Spirit is guiding us on the path that leads to loving as Jesus loved.

Love is the distinguishing mark of the follower of Jesus— and the Spirit is developing the capacity to love within us.

Love: the Goal of the Spirit's Work in our Lives.

CHAPTER 5

The Fruit of the Spirit Is Joy

The fruit of the Spirit is joy. Love, joy, and peace go together. Joy and peace describe the emotional tone that the Spirit of God is nurturing within each of us as the followers of Jesus. Joy and peace are what set us free to love. The absence of joy and peace blocks our ability to love.

Emotional Tone: The Lens through Which We View Life

Emotional tone is probably an unexplored aspect for most of us. The emotional tone of our lives is the inner disposition out of which we naturally live. It is the emotional lens through which we view the events and relationships of our lives, which, in turn, governs how we react to those events and personal interactions. Our emotional tone is so much a part of us that it functions outside of our conscious awareness. Consequently, our perceptions of events or personal interactions and our reactions to them are automatic and unconscious. We don't think about them; we don't choose them. We just react.

Emotional tone is not a dimension of personality. It is not about being outgoing or reserved, an extravert or an introvert. It is not about being a people person or a task-oriented person. These aspects of personality are the channels through which the emotional tone of our lives flows.

Of course, emotional tone or disposition can vary, depending on the day, depending on the challenges and stressors of the day, depending on our energy level. Any of us can have "a bad day." But each of us has a basic disposition—a default emotional tone—out of which we naturally, unconsciously live.

The emotional tone of our lives has been shaped through our life experiences, particularly the events of our formative years. Our early life experiences conditioned how we view life's experiences, thereby shaping how we react to life's events and interactions. It is as though those early life experiences put a pair of colored lenses on us. The color or the emotional hue of those lenses determines how we view life's events

> **The lenses through which we view and react to life are colored by fear.**

and interactions. That perception then determines how we react to those events and interactions. Because of this conditioning, we view today's events and interactions through the lenses of our past experiences.

The unpleasant reality about the emotional tone of our

lives is that each one is shaped by fear. The lenses through which we view and react to life are colored by fear.

We were created with four foundational emotional-relational needs. We were created with the need to be safe, the need to belong, the need for a sense of power or ability, and the need to be valued. Each of these emotional needs has a corresponding fear associated with it. The need to be safe translates into the fear of being hurt. The need to belong, that is, to be connected and live in relationship, translates into the fear of being rejected or abandoned. The need to have a sense of power or ability translates into the fear of being inadequate or not measuring up, the fear of being powerless and vulnerable. The need to be valued or have significance translates into the fear of being "less than," insignificant, or unimportant.[12] These four deep-seated fears determine the emotional tone of our lives. Operating outside our awareness, they shape how we view and relate to others as well as how we react to life's events. As long as these old fears dominate our lives, we will live without joy.[13]

Early in my adult years, a college friend described me as intense and serious. I didn't see myself that way, but she did. She told me I didn't know how to play. She identified the emotional tone out of which I lived as being intense and serious. As I reflected on her statement, I came to recognize the serious tone with which I approached life. Further reflection revealed the fear of failure that drove me to be so serious. My intense nature was a part of my drive to succeed. I did not want to fail or be perceived as a failure. This fear of failure reflects the need to be valued and the corresponding fear of being devalued and insignificant. Consequently, the emotional tone of my life had the face of focused intensity.

I have a friend who is just the opposite of my serious disposition. He is a happy-go-lucky, go-with-the-flow kind of person. The emotional tone of his life is fun loving—at least on the surface. My friend has confessed to me that his fun-loving nature is a cover-up for his fear of not measuring up. His fun-loving disposition is a mask covering a deep-seated fear of not being good enough. The class clown, the prankster, the teaser, the one who always has a joke to tell are other examples of a fun-loving, playful disposition that sometimes masks a deeper fear.

Some people are described as having a sweet disposition, a caring disposition, or a loving disposition. Even these "positive" dispositions can be rooted in the fear of being abandoned or rejected. The sweet, caring, or loving spirit was cultivated in order to avoid making other people angry.

Some people have angry dispositions. They are like porcupines. Every time you get too close, you catch a barb of anger. The emotional tone of their lives—the disposition they exude—is one of anger. Others are fearful people. Anxiety and worry dominate their lives. Anxiety and fear are the emotional tone out of which they live. The Disney character Piglet, in the Winnie the Pooh series, depicts such a fearful emotional tone. Eeyore, also in the Winnie the Pooh series, captures the emotional tone of depression. The lens through which such people view life is a negative, fear-based one that struggles to see anything good.

Some people who live out of fear do not come across as

fearful. Rather, they come across as strong and in charge. Strong personalities are often prone to be controlling and willful. Beneath the strength they exhibit lies a need to be in control. The emotional tone of their lives is one of strength, but underneath is the need to be in control, rooted in fear. The fear may be one of being out of control and, thereby, being in a position to be hurt or it may be a fear of being inadequate and not measuring up.

We've all known people who are critical and judgmental. They are always finding fault with someone or something. They look down on the other as though the other was inadequate and flawed. A judgmental spirit is the emotional tone of their lives. Jesus referred to the judgmental spirit as seeing the speck in another's eye while having a log in one's own eye.[14] His teaching suggests that the judgmental spirit is tied to blindness to one's own failings. The judgmental spirit masks a fear of facing one's own inadequacies.

Each of these examples—and certainly there are many more—are ways we have been conditioned to live. They are the emotional lens through which we unconsciously view life and, consequently, react to life. They are the fear-based disposition out of which we automatically deal with life's events.

Joy: The Emotional Tone of the Follower of Jesus

The Spirit is working to make joy the emotional tone in the life of every one of the followers of Jesus. Joy is the governing disposition out of which the follower of Jesus is destined to live.

Joy is a condition of the heart. It is a dimension of the interior realm of one's life, an inner reality that flows from the depths of one's being. Because it is an inner reality, joy is independent of external circumstances. It is not dependent upon the events of our lives. The biblical witness is that joy can be experienced in the midst of life's stress, life's challenges, and life's pain.

> The Spirit is working to make joy the emotional tone in the life of every follower of Jesus.

Joy is an inner disposition marked by freedom, openness, and delight. The spirit that knows joy is free from the life-restricting power of anxiety and fear. It relishes the goodness of life as a gift from the hand of God. Joy helps us recognize the gifts of God's goodness and blessing, wrapped in the wonder of creation, in the richness of relationships, and even in the challenge of life's events. Joy leads us to anticipate and look for that goodness. Even in the face of challenge and pain, joy creates openness to the goodness God will send and the blessings others will bring.

Joy is rooted in peace. Peace is that quietness of the heart and mind that allows us to experience joy. We experience peace as the Spirit leads us beyond the control of our deep-seated fears into resting in God's grace, faithfulness, and goodness. [15] We cannot experience joy without resting in God's peace. In the next chapter, we'll look more at peace as joy's companion and partner.

Joy displaces the fear-based emotional tone that was fashioned within us by our early experiences of life's events and relationships. In doing so, the Spirit heals us emotionally, breaking the power that our deep-seated fear holds over us. The Spirit moves us beyond fear and anxiety, beyond anger and depression, beyond negativity and a critical spirit, beyond being overly serious and the need to control.

The Spirit is performing a lens transplant in our lives, installing a different set of lenses through which to view life. The Spirit is training us to view life's events through the lenses of God's goodness, grace, and faithfulness. This God-shaped perspective allows us to see beyond what is. It helps us see beyond the current situation with its challenges, stress, and pain. This God-shaped set of lenses opens our eyes to see beyond what we fear life's events will do *to* us to see what God is doing *in* us through the experience. The Spirit gives us the eyes to see God and God's work.

This new set of lenses allows us to respond differently to life's events. The Spirit empowers us to respond out of the perspective of faith. We respond out of a quiet confidence in God's faithfulness rather than reacting out of fear. We respond, trusting God to provide strength in the midst of the challenge, to sustain us as we walk through it, and to bring out of the challenge blessings and growth we could not experience in any other way.

This change in the way we view life's events and in how we respond to them allows joy to flow from deep within us. We experience the joy of the Lord.[16] Joy becomes the emotional tone out of which we live. Joy becomes the Spirit-shaped outlook through which we view life. That joy, rooted in peace, sets us free to love as Jesus loved.

Joy: The Fruit of the Spirit

Joy is the fruit *of the Spirit*. It is a condition of the heart that the Spirit produces within us.

Joy is not something we can manufacture in our own strength. We can manufacture pleasure or entertainment or excitement or fun. All of these are tied to things outside us. We can pursue them by manipulating those things that foster them, but we cannot manufacture joy.

While we cannot manufacture joy, we *can* place ourselves in a position for the Spirit to work in our lives. We can open ourselves to the Spirit so the Spirit can produce love, joy, and peace within us. The following chapters will identify how to do so.

This chapter raises the question: what is the emotional tone of my life? The path that leads to loving as Jesus loves involves recognizing and naming the emotional tone of our lives.

The fruit of the Spirit is love, joy, and peace. The Spirit is cultivating joy and peace as the emotional tone of our lives so that we can love as Jesus loved.

Joy is the Spirit-shaped outlook through
which we view life. That joy, rooted in peace,
sets us free to love as Jesus loved.

Chapter 6

The Fruit of the Spirit Is Peace

The fruit of the Spirit is peace. Peace is joy's companion and partner. Peace is what allows joy to flow within us and through us. Together, joy and peace set us free to love as Jesus loved. In this grouping of three (love, joy, peace), peace is foundational.

Both Jesus and Paul spoke of peace. In John 14:27, Jesus said, "Peace I leave with you; my peace I give to you. I do not give to you as the world gives." In his letter to the Philippians, Paul spoke of "the peace of God which surpasses all understanding," (Philippians 4:7). Both Jesus and Paul spoke of the unusual nature of the peace that comes from God. Paul described it as a peace that cannot be understood or explained from a human perspective. Jesus described it as a different kind of peace than what the world gives.

The peace of Christ is an inner reality. It is something we experience deep within, at the core of our being. It is an inner quietness, a deep-seated sense of well-being and safety.

Anxiety and Fear: Barriers to Peace

The flip side of peace is anxiety and fear. Anxiety is a nebulous feeling of unease or dis-ease that lies just beneath the surface of our lives. We are most aware of it when we are in a situation in which we feel out of control. Anxiety is tied to our past experiences of fear, especially those associated with our formative years. Those experiences taught us to live in anticipation of things in life that would hurt us. They trained us to be on the lookout for what might happen next. The nebulous feeling of unease in life is the unconscious anticipation of something else that will hurt us. It is the twitching of the old fears identified in chapter 4: the fear of being hurt, the fear of being rejected and abandoned, the fear of being inadequate and powerless, the fear of being devalued and insignificant. This anxiety, when triggered, gives birth to fear.

Fear is that sense of alarm that we experience whenever we perceive something or someone as a threat. Fear is associated with a present threat or that which is perceived as a threat. The threat does not have to be real for fear to be triggered—just perceived.

Anxiety and fear are normal emotional reactions that occur inside us. Their role is to protect us from danger. They are what prompt us to unconsciously act in ways to avoid danger and keep ourselves safe. But these life-protecting abilities also stir inner restlessness and dis-ease that lead to the panicky need to do something.

Peace, what Jesus called "my peace," is what quietens

the anxiety with its nebulous feeling of dis-ease. It displaces the fear, stilling the inner turmoil and settling the inner restlessness. The peace of Christ sets us free from the power of anxiety and fear, breaking their control over us. It sets us free from fear-based thinking and fear-based reactivity. It displaces our anxiety and fear—in the midst of the very situation that spawned the fear in the first place!

This inner quietness we call peace comes *from* God. It is referred to as the fruit of the Spirit, the peace that Christ gives, and the peace of God. But it is also *rooted in* God. It is inseparably tied to God's faithfulness, what the Hebrew Bible calls the *faithful love of God*. It is tied to God's promise to be with us and not abandon us, to God's promise to bless us and sustain us. It is rooted in God's power to transform our experiences, bringing life out of death and good out of evil. It is tied to how God uses life's painful, destructive experiences to enrich and deepen our lives, maturing us in the likeness of Jesus.

The World's Kind of Peace

Our experience of being hurt by life's events and relationships taught us to deal with anxiety and fear in two distinct ways. These common ways of seeking peace produce the world's kind of peace.

First, we learned to focus on the perceived threat. We learned to focus outside ourselves, on that "out there" that we feared would hurt us. We all know the classic patterns of fear-based reaction: fight, flight, or freeze. Fight is the way of the badger. It attacks the threat, seeking to eliminate it by dominating it or destroying it. Flight is the way of the gazelle or deer. It runs away in an effort to escape the danger. Freeze is the way of the turtle. Feeling powerless to deal with or escape the threat, it withdraws into some kind of shell until the threat goes away. The focus of each of these reactive patterns is external, on that "out there" that appears threatening.

The second way we learned to deal with anxiety and fear was through control. All of us, in one way or another, attempt to be in control. We seek to control our circumstances, our health, our kids, and others. We attempt to control everything but ourselves. When we experience fear, we naturally attempt to control the "out there" that poses the threat. We attempt to be in control and avoid anything that might threaten to hurt us. Being in control is what makes us feel safe.

Our efforts to control do not produce an authentic sense of safeness or peace. The best our efforts to control can produce is predictability that has the appearance of stability. We create predictable routines and familiar patterns, designed to help us feel safe. In other words, we create comfort zones. However, our comfort zones offer, at best, a false sense of safeness and a false sense of peace. The peace they offer is tentative at best. It is tentative because we have no control over what life brings us.[17] In spite of our best efforts to be in control, life happens. The harsh realities of life still occur. We mistake stability and predictability for peace, but they are not real peace.

The world's kind of peace is tied to external things; the peace of Christ is tied to God. The world's kind of peace is tied to being in control; the peace of Christ is tied to God's faithfulness. The world's kind of peace is dependent on the situation and circumstances; the peace of Christ can be experienced in the midst of threatening circumstances. The way we learned to deal with anxiety and fear was to seek to avoid them by being in control; the peace of Christ quietens the anxiety and displaces the fear as we learn to exercise self-control.

The Journey into Peace

Peace is what the Spirit produces in our lives. Like the other traits in the fruit of the Spirit, peace is not something we can manufacture or produce through self-effort. It is not something we can create or conjure up. It is the product of the Spirit's work in our lives. While we cannot manufacture peace, we *can* place ourselves in a position for the Spirit to lead us into peace within.

The journey into peace begins with the *awareness* of the lack of peace. One would think that the recognition of this inner dis-ease we call anxiety would be easy, but it is not. Anxiety and fear are automatic reactions within us. They happen without our thinking and, thus, are outside our awareness. We have to learn to be aware of our anxiety and recognize our fear.

We learn to recognize our anxiety and fear by recognizing

what we commonly do when we are anxious and afraid. These old patterns of behavior are our unconscious attempts to reduce our sense of anxiety.

These reactions are different for each of us. Our individual patterns were developed early in life and refined through repeated use through the years. Some of us, when we are anxious and afraid, react with anger, and others attempt to run away. Some of us live as powerless victims, seeking someone to rescue us, and others jump in to take charge. Anxiety drives some of us to take care of others, and others withdraw into ourselves. Some of us fixate on the problem, allowing our minds to race with thoughts about what to do, and others simply shut down as though we were powerless.[18] Identifying our common pattern of fear-based reactivity puts us in a position to recognize it whenever the anxiety and fear kick in. That awareness comes from the Spirit and is the Spirit's invitation to the journey that leads to peace.

Having recognized the inner turmoil, the second step on the journey into peace is to manage the anxiety and fear. In John 14:27, Jesus promised his peace. In that same text, he also instructed, "Do not let your hearts be troubled and do not let them be afraid." In his letter to the Philippians, Paul exhorted them, "Do not worry about anything" (Philippians 4:6). The original language in both texts carries the idea of *stop—do not continue*. Fear and anxiety are a normal part of the human condition. They arise automatically in the face of perceived threats. Jesus's and Paul's words do not instruct us to *not* feel the anxiety and fear. Such is not possible. Rather, they call us to not dwell in our anxiety and fear. "Do not continue to live in your fear, with your fear, and out of your fear." They call us to move beyond our fear so that our fear does not dictate and control our lives.

Jesus and Paul called us to use our power to be in control. They called us to be in control of ourselves!

Rather than attempting to control others or our situation, we control ourselves. We manage what we are feeling along

Jesus and Paul call us to use our power to be in control of ourselves!

with the thinking that drives those feelings. We continue to live in fear and with fear only when we scare ourselves with our thinking. We scare ourselves when we focus on the uncertainty of the future, when we anticipate the worse, when we continually ask, "What if?"[19]

The recognition of our anxiety and fear presents us with a choice. Do we continue to hold onto our fear (allowing it to hold onto us) or choose to move beyond it? Do we live out of our fear or choose to let go of it?

When we hold onto fear, we give it control over us. It holds us in its grip. It shapes our thinking and governs what we do. Consequently, we react out of old patterns. Although these old patterns are unconscious and automatic, we can, through the work of the Spirit, move beyond them. We can choose to manage anxiety and fear rather than giving into them. We can put ourselves in a position for the Spirit to work within us. We do those things that allow the Spirit to displace our anxiety with peace and create an inner quietness in the place of our inner turmoil.

We do not manage anxiety and fear by fighting them, resisting them, or seeking to control them. We manage our anxiety and fears by naming them. We acknowledge them to God. We pray. The journey into peace follows the path of prayer.

Through prayer, we remember, refocus, and reconnect with God so that we can rest in God's faithful love. Prayer is the way we manage our fears.

> **The journey into peace follows the path of prayer.**

In his letter to the Philippians, Paul wrote, "Do not worry about anything, but in everything by prayer and supplication with thanksgiving let your requests be made known to God." Paul didn't just say, "Don't worry." He exhorted the Philippian disciples to manage their anxiety and fear. "Don't continue to worry. You're doing it. Stop!" And, then, he told them how to move beyond the worry into peace. He instructed them to pray. Pray the fear. Acknowledge it. Express it. Bring your requests to God. Paul also instructed the Philippians in how to pray. They were to pray with thanksgiving.

Thanksgiving is rooted in remembering. It is looking over our shoulders at the past, remembering God's faithfulness in past situations. Thanksgiving is the key to moving beyond fear-based praying. Thanksgiving helps us remember God and God's faithfulness. It helps us remember how God was with us even when we couldn't recognize God's presence. It helps us remember how God strengthened and sustained us in the midst of our crisis. Thanksgiving helps us remember how God provided what we needed to deal with the crisis. It helps us remember how God transformed the experience to bring good out of evil and life out of death. Thanksgiving helps us recognize how God blessed us and matured us as we walked a road we would rather have not walked. Praying with thanksgiving helps us remember. And, when we remember, we are in a position to reconnect with God.

Our fear and anxiety blind us to God. When we are living out of anxiety and fear, our attention is on the situation. We are focused on the circumstances and on others and on what we are afraid might happen. In other words, our focus is not on God. In the midst of our anxiety and fear, the Spirit calls us to refocus on God and, thereby, reconnect with God.

The Spirit guides us to remember so we can refocus. As we refocus on God, we can reconnect with God. When we reconnect with God, we can then rest in God.

Remember → Refocus → Reconnect → Rest

The Spirit leads us to rest in God's faithful love. Resting involves choosing to let go of our fear and our need to be in control. It involves choosing to trust. This Spirit-directed remembering, this Spirit-directed refocusing, this Spirit-directed reconnecting, this Spirit-empowered resting allows us to experience deep within the kind of peace that surpasses all human ability to understand or explain it.[20]

This journey into peace is not some magic formula that automatically makes everything better. It is a process—a journey.

The Journey into Peace

Become aware of the anxiety and inner dis-ease - the lack of peace

Manage the anxiety by naming it to God

Praying with thanksgiving, remember, refocus, and reconnect with God

Rest in God's faithful love, letting go of the anxiety and fear

It is a process of consciously shifting our focus from our situation to God, from frantically worrying about everything "out there" to managing what's "in here," from attempting to be in control to turning loose, from doing what we always do to resting. The journey into peace is choosing to live in relationship with God, trusting God's faithful love. It is choosing to live in glad dependency upon the Spirit.

Peace is that inner quietness in the depth of our being that allows the joy of the Lord to flow in us and through us. Peace and joy put us in a position to love as Jesus loved.

The connection of peace and joy to love reflects the reality stated above: how we treat others reflects the condition of our hearts. When our hearts are full of anxiety and fear, our relationships reflect the chaos reflected in the works of the flesh (Galatians 5:19–21). When we live out of peace and joy, we are set free to love as Jesus loved. We relate with patience, kindness, generosity, faithfulness, and gentleness.

Peace and joy are foundational for relating out of grace.

Joy and Peace: the Spirit out of Which Love Flows

CHAPTER 7

The Fruit of the Spirit Is Grace-Based Relationships

The next five traits of the fruit of the Spirit are all relational terms: patience, kindness, generosity, faithfulness, and gentleness. These five traits go together as a subgroup within the nine. Just as love, joy, and peace are a subgroup describing the inner disposition or emotional tone the Spirit cultivates in our lives, so this group of five identifies how the Spirit empowers us to live in relationship. These five help us see what love looks like. They are how love is expressed as we live in relationship with another.

Each of these five traits is an expression of grace. When we live out of these traits, we move beyond what we believe the other deserves. These five traits are what relating out of grace and forgiveness looks like.

Slow Driver in the Passing Lane:
A Parable about the Flesh

I enjoy road trips on our nation's interstate highways. I enjoy seeing the countryside as well as the solitude the car provides. My sense of enjoyment is disturbed, however, by someone driving slow in the fast lane. State law designates the far-left lane as a passing lane. Slower traffic is to keep right except when passing. It's the law! And the law is posted on road signs along the interstate: "Slower Traffic Keep Right!"

Whenever I come up behind a driver who is driving slowly in the passing lane, my reaction is predictable. I become impatient and frustrated. The longer I am stuck behind this driver, the more irritated and anxious I become. Criticalness surges to the surface, spawning demeaning thoughts and words toward the other. I view the other as ignorant, not knowing the law, or as so self-absorbed that they are insensitive to others. (How often is this slow driver talking on their cell phone, completely oblivious to the traffic behind them!) And I am justified in my (superior!) attitude because the driver is not only breaking the law, they are creating a danger as traffic piles up behind them. My frustration and irritation are only relieved when I find a way to get around them, generally by passing them on the right.

Impatience is a normal part of the human condition. It is a reaction we all experience. That which triggers our impatience differs for each of us, but the *pattern* of our reaction is the same. We become frustrated, angry, and anxious because life is not unfolding the way we want it to be. We are critical of the other—with no thought of the other or the other's situation or need—because our focus in only on ourselves and what we want. We act from a posture of superiority in which we know what is best (and the other is not doing it!). We emotionally distance ourselves from the other with harsh, demeaning thoughts, words, and, sometimes, actions.

This pattern of reaction is universal and predictable. And it is toxic. It creates chaos in relationships while robbing us of peace and joy. This pattern is an expression of what Paul called *the flesh*, that self-focused, self-serving spirit that is inherent to our human condition. The reactions in this pattern are expressions of earning-deserving thinking and relating.[21]

Paul seemingly understood this common human experience since he described just the opposite in the five relational traits in the fruit of the Spirit.

How Love Is Expressed in Relationships

Love is expressed in our relationships when we live out of patience, kindness, generosity, faithfulness, and gentleness.

The first of the five relational traits is *patience*. The word Paul used expresses the idea of suffering long in a relationship. It means to put up with or to bear with the other when the other is not easy to deal with or pleasant to be around. Patience is the expression of a compassionate, understanding spirit that sees beyond what the other does to what is expressed in what the other is doing.

The Spirit empowers the follower of Jesus to be patient. Impatience is the normal expression of our default human nature, *the flesh*. Impatience is a form of anger. We generally experience it as frustration or irritation. Impatience is always tied to our expectations. We become frustrated and irritated whenever the other does not do what we want them to do or does not do what we think is right (such as driving slow in the passing lane). We become impatient whenever the other does not do things "my way." The underlying attitude is "My way is right. I know better. If you would just do it my way, then ..." Every time we are impatient with another, we are expressing a not-so-subtle arrogance. We are acting like a judge who judges the other for not doing what is "right." We are playing God and attempting to shape the world the way "I want it to be."

The fruit of the Spirit is patience. Impatience is an expression of the flesh.

Whenever we are impatient, how we view and treat the other becomes negative. Our touch on their lives is harsh and hurtful. By contrast, patience leads us to be *kind* in how we treat the other. Kindness and gentleness go together. Kindness is the attitude or spirit with which we view and relate to others. Gentleness is how we use our power to touch them. Kindness involves being thoughtful. It is the ability to see and relate from another's perspective. Thus, it moves beyond thinking only from our own expectations and desires to considering the other's needs and desires.

In contrast to kindness, the flesh is critical and condemning. Whenever the other does not measure up to our expectations or do things "my way," we become judgmental. This critical, judgmental spirit is harsh and insensitive, the opposite of being kind. We find fault with the other and what they do. Not only do we view them as not measuring up, we deem them to be flawed and inadequate, as though something is wrong with them. We treat them accordingly. We relate to them out of anger with a condescending attitude, angry looks, and a reprimanding, demeaning tone. We put them down as though they were worthless or less than. Our critical stance moves us from being the judge to being the judge, jury, and executioner all rolled into one. This kind of judgmental spirit reflects our preoccupation with our own interests and desires.

The fruit of the spirit is kindness. The flesh expresses itself in critical, judgmental spirit and condemning, condescending behavior.

Kindness is expressed in *generosity*. Generosity is about giving. It speaks of a spirit that gives freely, abundantly, and even lavishly. One who is generous gives to the other from what one has to address what the other needs. Generosity begins with giving one's time and attention by being totally present with the other. It does the hard work of hearing the other. It also involves giving patience and understanding and forgiveness. Generosity involves giving of one's abilities, knowledge, gifts, and resources to help the other. The result of generosity is a grace-filled touch on the other's life that addresses the other's need.

By contrast, the flesh operates out of a calculating, stingy spirit. Our inherent self-serving spirit functions out of a perspective of scarcity. This spirit leads us to withhold what we have to give. It almost always is rooted in earning-deserving thinking. We judge the other as not worthy or deserving of our time, attention, patience, kindness, understanding, compassion, forgiveness, or help. We make no effort to understand the other or the other's position. We simply judge and, thus, withhold from the other what God has entrusted to us.

The fruit of the spirit is generosity. The flesh expresses itself in a calculating, stingy spirit that withholds from the other, robbing them of what they need.

Generosity in inseparably linked to *faithfulness.* Just as kindness and gentleness go together, so generosity and faithfulness go together. Faithfulness means we refuse to give up on a relationship or abandon the other. We stay in the relationship, refusing to walk away, when the relationship becomes difficult. Faithfulness is to be patient with the other and kind to the other, giving of self to help the other, to work through issues to healing and growth.

By contrast, the flesh leads us to withdraw from those with whom we find fault. We create emotional distance, holding ourselves aloof from the other as though we were better than them. We choose to not have anything to do with them. We seek to avoid them so that we don't have to deal with them. We physically withdraw from them. Sometimes we go so far as to cut them out of our lives, in essence, throwing them away.

The fruit of the spirit is faithfulness. When we react out

of the flesh, we give up on people and discard them as not worth our time or energy or effort.

Gentleness is the partner of kindness. Gentleness is about how we use our power and, thereby, how we touch the other. Gentleness is a touch filled with grace. The touch may be with our hands or with our words, with our attitude or our looks, or with our behavior and actions. Gentleness touches the other in ways that do not leave a bruise or mark, in ways that do not wound or hurt, and in ways that do not cause or add to the other's pain and struggle.

The word translated as gentleness can also be translated as humility. Humility is the awareness of our own humanness and weakness, of our own struggle and failure, and, thus, of our own need for grace. This awareness leads us to be understanding and compassionate, gentle and kind, in how we respond to others' humanness, weakness, and struggle. Gentleness looks beyond the behavior or the situation to the hurt beneath the surface. It gently touches the other in a way that soothes and eases the pain, lifts the burden, and helps heal the hurt.

The reaction of the flesh is always hard and harsh, the opposite of gentleness. Such harshness is expressed through our attitudes, our looks, and our tones of voice. It is expressed in the way we speak to the other and about the other. It is expressed in how we treat the other. Our touch on the other's life is hard. Because the flesh operates out of earning-deserving thinking, we use our power to punish the other by inflicting some form of pain on them.[22] Rather than a gentleness born of humility, we view the other out of our arrogance as though we know what is wrong with the other and what they need to do to get their act together. We justify the harsh way we touch them by focusing on their inadequacies. Ironically, our focus on their failings blinds us to our own.

The fruit of the spirit is gentleness; the reaction of the flesh is always hard and harsh, wounding and destructive.

The Fruit of the Spirit versus the Pattern of the Flesh

The fruit of the Spirit and the pattern of the flesh portray two radically different ways of relating to others.

The fruit of the Spirit relates out of grace. Grace sees the other through the eyes of God. It leads us to accept the other unconditionally and forgive freely. As a dimension of love, grace seeks the good of the other. This desire for the other's wholeness leads the follower of Jesus to give of oneself as a servant. That giving is expressed in patience, kindness, generosity, faithfulness, and gentleness.

The flesh, our default human nature, relates out of earning-deserving thinking. It is quick to give the other what their weaknesses and failures deserve. Operating out of an arrogant posture, the flesh is impatience, irritable, critical, and condemning. It lives out of a stingy, calculating spirit that is quick to give up on people and throw them away. It is harsh and hard in the way it touches the other, always leaving a mark or bruise or wound.

The pattern of the flesh happens automatically, beyond

our awareness and with no conscious thought involved. The fruit of the Spirit requires conscious choosing as we will see in the next chapter.

The pattern of the flesh is rooted in anxiety and fear. When we are anxious, full of angst and inner turmoil, we focus on ourselves. We live out of a self-serving, what's-in-it-for-me spirit. Our needs and desires take priority. As a result, we are impatient, critical, and judgmental of others. We withhold what they need and tend to give up on them. Our touch on their lives tends to be hard, harsh, uncaring.

By contrast, the fruit of the Spirit arises out of inner joy and peace. Joy and peace set us free to be patient and kind, generous and faithful, and gentle. The Spirit empowers us to love as Jesus loved.

Grace-Based Relating: The Fruit of the Spirit

It is common for us to say, "I need to be more patient." The same could be said of being kind or generous or faithful or gentle, but we generally focus on being more patient. This common form of self-judgment is a needed reminder regarding the fruit of the Spirit. In these five relational traits, Paul was not describing a set of "oughts" to which we "need to" conform. If we approach these five traits out of the spirit of "I ought to ..." or "I should be more ...," we are missing Paul's point.

This grace-based way of relating is not something we can do through self-effort. These are not ideals we aspire to by trying harder to do better. No amount of self-effort will produce these traits. These traits are the fruit of the Spirit. They are what the Spirit produces within us as we learn to walk in the Spirit. They are real possibilities that we can experience in our lives and in our relationships today—but only through the power of the Spirit!

Because the flesh is our default nature, we will continue to be impatient as we judge others by our expectations. We will be critical and judgmental of them. We will withhold our compassion and understanding, our patience and forgiveness. We will emotionally distance ourselves from them and even seek to avoid them. We will touch them with our attitudes, our looks, our tones of voice, and our actions in ways that wound and hurt. The good news is that we do not have to continue to live out of this old pattern of the flesh. Our *recognition* that we are doing so is the Spirit's work within us, calling us to place ourselves in a position for the Spirit to lead us into joy and peace so that we are set free to love as Jesus loved.

The ability to love as Jesus loved, what I have called *grace-based relating*, is possible through the ninth trait the Spirit produces within us. Self-control is the key to loving as Jesus loved.

Patience, Kindness, Generosity, Faithfulness, and Gentleness: What Love Looks like in Relationships

CHAPTER 8

The Fruit of the Spirit Is Self-control

Is it really possible for us to love as Jesus loved? Jesus taught his disciples that love is the distinguishing characteristic of his followers, but can we really love as Jesus loved? Is it possible in our lives today?

My sense is that most of us, if we were honest, would say no. We are deeply aware of our default human nature—what Paul called *the flesh*. We are intimately familiar with the pattern of the flesh described in chapter 7. We commonly struggle and generally fail in our efforts to be more patient or more loving. Our struggle leads us to believe that loving as Jesus loved is beyond our ability. We're too human to love as he loved.

Believing that we cannot love as Jesus loved excuses us from having to do so. So, instead of love, we generally use something else to identify ourselves as the followers of Jesus. We substitute something else for love. One of the most common substitutes is right belief.

Churches and Christians today commonly identify themselves by what they believe about the Bible or about

Jesus as the way to heaven. This substitute is also seen in the stance some take on moral issues such as abortion, LBGTQ[23] issues, and immigration, the hot topics of the day. Others use religious practices and church involvement to identify themselves as the followers of Jesus. Many pride themselves on giving financially to help those they deem to be "the less fortunate" and in their involvement in mission trips beyond their neighborhoods.[24] None of these substitutes require us to love as Jesus loved. In fact, some of these beliefs and practices are expressed in ways that reflect the critical, judgmental pattern of the flesh rather than the love that Jesus said was the distinguishing characteristic of his followers.

The reality is that we cannot love as Jesus loved—in our own strength. All of these things we substitute for love are things we can do with our own strength. We don't need God's help to hold on to right belief or a particular stance on a moral issue, but we need God's help to love as Jesus loved. We need the Spirit's guidance and power to be patient and kind, generous and faithful, and gentle.

The apostle Paul understood that we, as the followers of Jesus, could love as Jesus loved. He also understood that such love was only possible through the work of the Spirit in our lives. His description of the fruit of the Spirit identified the path that leads us to loving as Jesus loved.

The key to loving as Jesus loved lies in the ninth trait Paul listed in the fruit of the Spirit. The first trait, love, identifies the goal that the Spirit is seeking to produce

> **The key to loving as Jesus loved lies in Spirit-empowered self-control.**

within us. The Spirit is working to empower us to love as Jesus loved. The last trait, self-control, is the key to doing so. Self-control is the one trait that makes the other eight possible. Spirit-empowered self-control is what allows us to rest in God's peace so that the joy of the Lord can flow in us and through us. That joy and peace set us free to be patient and kind, generous and faithful, and gentle in how we relate to others. Joy and peace set us free to love. The key to loving as Jesus loved lies in Spirit-empowered self-control.

Spirit-Empowered Self-Control

What is this self-control of which Paul speaks? It is common to think of self-control in terms of behavior. We exercise self-control to watch what we eat or how much we eat. We pass on dessert or limit our portions. We exercise self-control when we come across a great sale but choose not to spend the money. We exercise self-control when we bite our tongues to keep from saying what we are thinking. Those of us in recovery exercise self-control by not reverting to old addictions and patterns of behavior. Some of us exercise self-control by controlling what we do when we are angry. Some of us think of self-control as relating primarily to sexual desires. Each of these is an example of self-control, but none of these expressions of self-control help us love as Jesus loved.

When Paul spoke of self-control, he was thinking of more than controlling our physical appetites and desires, more than controlling our behavior and choices. His focus was something much deeper, something deep within, out of which our behaviors flow.

Paul's understanding of self-control was rooted in the reality that how we treat others is an expression of what lies in our hearts. Our relationships reflect what is in our hearts and minds. How we view and treat others in any given moment is determined by whether our hearts are full of anxiety or peace, frustration or joy. The interior realm determines the outside.

This reality is seen in the interrelatedness of the first three traits. Peace—that deep, inner quietness of the spirit—is what allows joy to flow in us and through us. Joy and peace then set us free to love. Relationships filled with patience, kindness, generosity, faithfulness, and gentleness flow out of a heart filled with joy and peace. The joy and peace that are in the heart are mirrored in how we relate to others.

> **How we view and treat others in any given moment is determined by whether our hearts are full of anxiety or peace, frustration or joy. Self-control is about managing what is in our hearts, i.e., the spirit out of which we live.**

The opposite is also true. When our heart is full of fear instead of peace, when it is full of frustration and angst instead of joy, that inner dis-ease will be reflected in how we view and treat others. Inner turmoil makes us self-absorbed. We become consumed with getting our own desires, wants, and needs met. Consequently, we are irritable instead of patient, critical and judgmental instead of kind, stingy and withholding instead of generous, emotionally aloof and withdrawn instead of faithful, and harsh and hard instead of gentle. What's on the inside determines how we view and treat others at that given moment.

This reality guides our understanding of what Paul meant by self-control. Self-control is about what lies in the heart, in the interior realm. Self-control is managing the spirit out of which we live.

The objective is to love as Jesus loved. Such love requires us to manage the spirit out of which we live. It requires that we exercise self-control.

Self-Control → Loving as Jesus Loved

But self-control requires self-awareness. We cannot manage the spirit out of which we live unless we are aware of it.

Self-awareness is being aware of what we are experiencing inside. It is being aware of the inner dis-ease that stirs within us. It is recognizing when we are anxious, afraid, frustrated, irritable, or angry. Being aware of what is churning inside presents us with a choice. We can continue to feel the anxiety, fear, frustration, and anger—or we can choose to manage it. If we continue to live with the inner turmoil, we will inevitably act out of it.[25] If we choose to manage what we are feeling, we can then choose to respond differently, in a way more in line with the teachings of Jesus. Self-awareness gives us the opportunity to practice self-control. If we are not aware of our inner dis-ease, we will automatically act out of it. We will act without thinking.

Self-awareness involves the mind; self-control involves the will. Self-control is an exercise of the will. It is choosing to manage what we feel and think so that we can choose how we will respond. In exercising self-control, we stop our old ways of reacting and choose to follow the ways of God that Jesus taught.

Choosing is an exercise of the will. This opportunity to choose—to practice self-control—is possible because of self-awareness. Self-awareness is the work of the intellect. Self-awareness is recognizing when the old fears are raging because the old issues have been touched. Self-awareness, like self-control, is an ability the Spirit cultivates within us.

Self-Awareness → Self-Control → Loving as Jesus Loved

Self-awareness is grounded in self-understanding. The more we know ourselves, the greater our ability to live with self-awareness. Self-understanding involves knowing what triggers the anxiety, fear, frustration, and angst within. These triggers are generally related to our deep-seated fears: the fear of being hurt, the fear of being rejected or abandoned, the fear of being inadequate and powerless, or the fear of being devalued and insignificant. Self-understanding also involves knowing how we normally react when we feel anxiety and angst. The more I know myself, the more I am able to recognize when these old patterns are triggered within me.[26]

Self-Understanding → Self-Awareness → Self-Control → Loving as Jesus Loved

Exercising Self-Control: Managing the Spirit out of Which We Live

Don't miss Paul's point: exercising self-control is the work of the Spirit in our lives. Western culture has trained us to be fiercely independent and self-reliant. Any form of dependency is viewed as a weakness and failure.

This training gets carried over into our discipleship in our resolve to try harder to do better, but self-control is not something we can do in our own strength. It is not a matter of self-will or self-effort. No amount of trying harder to do better or of being more disciplined will produce self-control in our lives. Self-control is not a matter of being more committed or having more faith. Self-control is what the Spirit produces in us. It grows out of the Spirit's work in our lives as we walk in relationship with God.

The awareness of our inner dis-ease is the work of the Spirit. This self-awareness is the Spirit's call to manage the spirit out of which we are living *in that moment*. Self-awareness is the Spirit's call to turn to God for strength beyond our own. It is a call to open ourselves to the Spirit's work. Self-awareness is a call to prayer. Through prayer, we put ourselves in a position for the Spirit to replace anxiety, fear, frustration, and angst with peace.

Breath Prayer: The Path to Self-Control

I have found *breath prayer* to be an effective way to open myself to the Spirit's work. Breath prayer involves using our breathing as the pattern of our prayer.

In breath prayer, we control our breathing. We breathe in deeply through the nose, hold our breath for three to five seconds, and then breathe out through our mouths. The controlled breathing is a vital part of the prayer experience. When we are full of anxiety, fear, frustration, or anger, we unconsciously feel out of control. Controlling our breathing—something we normally do without thinking— gives us a sense of being in control of ourselves![27]

As we follow this pattern of controlled breathing, we pray. As we breathe in, we pray, "Fill me, Spirit of God." As we exhale, we pray, "Cleanse me." Thus, we pray away our anxiety, fear, frustration, and anger. "Fill me with your peace; cleanse me of my anxiety and fear. Fill me with your joy; cleanse me of my frustration and anger."

Through this pattern of prayer, we place ourselves in a position for the Spirit to address our internal dis-ease.

Choosing to pray away anxiety, fear, frustration, or anger is exercising self-control. We don't control the anxiety, fear, frustration, or anger. We place ourselves in a position for *the Spirit* to displace them and lead us into peace. As the peace of Christ displaces our inner dis-ease, joy can flow in us and through us. Joy and peace set us free to choose to love as Jesus loved.

Self-control is managing the spirit out of which we live. It involves choosing to pray our internal turmoil and inner disease, placing ourselves in a position for the Spirit to displace our anxiety with peace, our frustration with joy. Out of that joy and peace, we can then—and only then—choose to be patient and kind, generous and faithful, and gentle in the way we relate to others.

We *can* love as Jesus loved—through the work and power of the Spirit!

The Spirit is working within us to empower us to love as Jesus loved. The starting point of that work is empowering us to manage the spirit out of which we live. Spirit-empowered self-control is the key to loving as Jesus loved.

Self-control: the Key to Loving as Jesus Loved

CHAPTER 9

Keep in Step with the Spirit

Two exhortations bracket the apostle Paul's teaching about the fruit of the Spirit. The opening exhortation is "live by the Spirit" (Galatians 5:16). The Spirit, not the Law, guides us in living as the followers of Jesus. The Spirit leads us beyond the reactive patterns of our default human nature, the flesh, while filling our lives with the fruit of the Spirit. Given this transformative work of the Spirit, Paul urged his readers (us!) to keep in step with the Spirit so that the Spirit's transforming work might be a reality in their lives. "Since we live by the Spirit, let us keep in step with the Spirit" (5:25 NIV).[28]

The phrase "since we live by the Spirit" is a reference to the opening exhortation in 5:16: "live by the Spirit." We live under the guidance of the Spirit, in glad dependency on the Spirit, looking to the Spirit for the power to do what we cannot do in our own strength, knowing the Spirit will lead us to love as Jesus loved. Given this Spirit-oriented and Spirit-dependent way of living, our efforts are to be focused on keeping in step with the Spirit. We are to follow as the

Spirit guides us so that our lives can be filled with the fruit of the Spirit and we can love as Jesus loved.

Dancing with the Spirit

Years ago, my wife and I took a series of dance lessons. That experience taught me that there is a lot more to dancing than getting on the dance floor when the music starts. The lessons began with teaching us the right steps. However, in order to be good dancers, we had to dance the right steps in rhythm with the music and in rhythm with each other. We had to lose ourselves in the music, moving with its tempo, while moving in rhythm with one another.

Living by the Spirit is much like learning to dance. Learning to dance begins with learning the steps to the dance. Similarly, learning the ways of God that Jesus taught is foundational to living by the Spirit. In order to guide us as the followers of Jesus, the Spirit teaches us the ways of the kingdom that Jesus taught. The Spirit then leads us to dance to the rhythm of God's love and forgiveness. Joy and peace become the emotional tone of our lives as the Spirit heals old wounds, silences old shame-based messages, and moves us beyond the fear-based reactions of our default nature.

One of the challenges in dancing is determining which of the partners leads. Keeping in step with the Spirit is following the Spirit's lead. The Spirit helps us recognize when joy and peace are disrupted by inner turmoil and dis-ease. We learn to identity that recognition as the Spirit's call to prayer.

Following the Spirit's guidance, we put ourselves in a position for the Spirit to help us manage the anxiety and fear, the negativity and angst, the frustration and anger that are boiling within. In the midst of anxiety-producing events and interactions, the Spirit guides us back into joy and peace so that we can choose to love as Jesus loved. The Spirit empowers us to exercise self-control, freeing us to respond to the other with patience, kindness, generosity, faithfulness, and gentleness *in the heat of the moment.*[29]

Learning to Dance with the Spirit

Living by the Spirit and keeping in step with the Spirit describe a way of living in relationship with God that is intensely personal and intimate. Like all aspects of the spiritual life, this quality of relationship can be nurtured and developed. It is a way of relating that we can learn and in which we can grow—as the Spirit guides us!

Living by the Spirit and keeping in step with the Spirit assume awareness of the Spirit's movement and work deep within. Awareness of and openness to the Spirit can be cultivated through spiritual practices that slow us down from the busyness of our doing-oriented nature and train us to focus on the interior realm of our lives.[30] We can learn to be still in the presence of God, quietening the myriad voices that fill our minds with the demands of responsibilities and tasks that await our attention. Cultivating these abilities fosters awareness of the Spirit through the day.

As would be expected, learning this alternate way of living is challenging. It involves unlearning old patterns and developing new ones. In this process of learning and growing, the Spirit will lead us beyond fear-based thinking and reacting to consciously choosing to live by faith in God's faithful love and abundance. The Spirit will lead us to surrender the arrogant spirit of being self-reliant and self-sufficient for a posture of confident humility[31] that lives in glad dependency upon the Spirit.

The Spirit will lead us to crucify[32] our sense of identity that we have constructed based upon what the world values and discover the person God created us to be. The Spirit will lead us to move beyond us-them thinking and relating with its underlying *better than, less than* attitudes and judgmental spirit so that we can embrace others with the radical hospitality and unconditional acceptance of Jesus. The Spirit will lead us each step of the way. Our role is to keep in step as the Spirit leads.

Out of Step with the Spirit

Until we learn to dance with the Spirit, following the Spirit's guiding nudges, we inevitably live out of our default nature. We live by *the flesh* and not the Spirit. We dance to the rhythm of our own will, following the fear-driven cravings of our desires and needs. We unconsciously react when our deep-seated fears are stirred. We live out of a competitive spirit rooted in us-them thinking. We naturally view ourselves as better than the other.

Paul warned the Galatians about this kind of relating: "Let us not become conceited, competing against one another, envying one another" (Galatians 5:26). Our competitive spirit often involves hostility toward and attacks against the other. "If, however, you bite and devour one another, take care that you are not consumed by one another" (Galatians 5:15). Ultimately, we experience the works of the flesh Paul identified (Galatians 5:19–21): self-indulgent lifestyles, obsession with power and control, and the chaos of conflict and broken relationships.

We attempt to temper the expressions of this default nature through our religious life. However, until we learn to live by the Spirit, religious life can become another way for the ego-oriented self to manifest itself. We view religious practices and church involvement as the indicators of our spirituality rather than as resources that lead to a spiritually transformed life. We emphasize beliefs and morals[33] rather than spiritual formation that results in being conformed to the likeness of Christ. We focus on conforming to religious standards rather than on the transformation of the heart. We substitute being good people and financially helping those we deem as less fortunate for loving as Jesus loved. We get trapped in self-effort, trying harder to do better, or we surrender to the mediocracy of "doing the best I can." In other words, *we do what we know how to do and what we can do in our own strength!* These patterns become ways we avoid doing what Jesus taught. This kind of religious life often becomes routine and stale, stunted and unfruitful, and lonely and empty.

Living by the Spirit and keeping in step with the Spirit leads us into spiritual vitality, into spiritual growth toward Christlike spiritual maturity, and into fruitfulness in a Spirit-guided ministry. The Spirit alone can lead us beyond our self-serving, default nature. The Spirit alone can guide us into joy and peace. The Spirit alone can free us to be patient and kind, generous and faithful, and gentle in how we relate to others. The Spirit alone can empower us to love as Jesus loved.

No wonder Paul exhorted the Galatian disciples to live by the Spirit and to keep in step with the Spirit. The Spirit guides us on the path that leads to loving as Jesus loved.

Keep in step with the Spirit!

CHAPTER 10

Anne's Story

A sharp pain pierced Anne's heart. Fred's words cut deeply.[34] "I heard some *good* preaching last Sunday while I was in Dallas." Fred emphasized the word "good" so that the message was unmistakable: he didn't consider Anne's preaching to be good.

Anne was Fred's pastor. That is, Anne was the pastor of the church of which Fred was a member. Anne had never felt that Fred had allowed her to be his pastor. He had been open in his opposition to having a woman as a pastor. He regularly questioned every decision she made, challenged her leadership, and never missed an opportunity to criticize her. And now he was openly attacking her preaching in a way that everyone within twenty feet could hear.

Fred was in his seventies. He had spent his adult years as an active leader in the church. However, age and health challenges had limited his ability to be as active as he had once been and had diminished his leadership role in the congregation. Other, younger members were filling positions he had long enjoyed and were making decisions he had once made. His wife of fifty-plus years had died just before Anne became pastor of the church.

Anne remained courteous as she struggled not to show her pain or react to it. "I am glad to hear that, Fred. Perhaps you can tell me about it sometime this week. Let's have coffee. It's good to have you back in worship today."

Anne had been working with a counselor-coach since coming to the church less than two years ago. She had specifically sought guidance about how to relate to Fred and about why he had such an ability to push her buttons. More than anyone in the congregation, he could leave her frustrated, discouraged, and hurting. Anne hated the power Fred seemed to have over her.

Through her work with her counselor-coach, Anne had gained greater self-understanding and was using that understanding to be more self-aware. Anne was the first of two children. Her younger brother was born just shy of her second birthday. Although she knew she was loved, Anne felt overshadowed by her younger brother. He was an outgoing extrovert; she was a shy introvert. He was athletic and active; she was more reflective and intuitive.

Some of her earliest memories were of her brother as a preschooler invading her room and getting into her things. When she complained, she was told that he didn't know better and was encouraged to share. Even at that early age, she heard the unspoken message: "He is more important. What you think and feel doesn't matter as much as what he wants."

Her sense of being devalued and *less than* was compounded

by the way her father's family treated her brother as "special." Her brother ensured the family name would continue. He even bore his father's and grandfather's name and was called Trey. As for her, she was just Anne—sweet Anne.

Anne learned early in life how to survive in the shadow of her brother. She learned to sacrifice what she felt, thought, or wanted to avoid making waves. "Go along to get along" became a guiding principle. She learned to stuff her feelings, especially any feelings of jealousy, anger, or resentment toward Trey. Such feelings stirred a deep sense of shame, leading her to believe that something was deeply flawed in her that she would feel such things about her brother. She learned to withdraw into herself—alone with her feelings of being flawed, inadequate, and insignificant.

Her feelings often led her into periods of depression that she carefully hid from her family. Her only sense of value came through her academic abilities. She enjoyed the praise she received when her report card was full of A's. She especially enjoyed the recognition she received from her teachers and school administrators by being her high school valedictorian and earning an academic scholarship to a prestigious out-of-state university. But even that accomplishment was overshadowed by her brother's role as the starting quarterback on the football team that went to the quarterfinals of the state playoffs.

Anne's counselor-coach helped her recognize the old issues along with the patterns she had developed to cope with them. She also helped Anne recognize how her relationship with Fred triggered those old issues. In Fred, she was once again being told by "family" that she was *less than*, inadequate, and not valued. This understanding gave Anne the opportunity to choose a different response rather than automatically reacting out of her old patterns.

Living with this self-understanding, Anne had learned to recognize the pain of the old issues when they surfaced (self-awareness) as it did when Fred made his critical, passive-aggressive comment about her preaching. That awareness gave her a choice. She could hold on to the pain and react in old ways or manage her pain and respond out of her commitment to live as a follower of Jesus. That way, she could love Fred as Jesus loved him.

In the moment of the interaction, Anne responded as best she could to Fred, drawing on the understanding she had gained through her work with her counselor-coach. When she was alone, Anne replayed the interaction with Fred. She listened again to his comment and felt the pain that it stirred. However, she refused to hold on to the pain. She chose to manage it. She prayed. Using the breath prayer, she prayed her pain saying, "Fill me; cleanse me. Fill me with your joy; cleanse me of my anger and hurt. Fill me with your peace; cleanse me of my anxiety about being *less than*. Fill me with your love for Fred; cleanse me of my need to protect my own ego."

Anne's prayer did not lead to immediate relief, but she continued to meditate and pray. She continued to place herself in a position for the Spirit to work in her. She continued to pray until clarity came, bringing peace. That clarity and peace freed her to respond to Fred differently. Relying on the

Spirit's power, she chose to be patient with Fred even though she felt irritated and frustrated by his behavior. She chose to be kind to him rather than being critical and judgmental of him. She chose to be understanding and forgiving, aware that he was walking through a painful, grief-filled time in his life. She chose not to distance herself from him or give up on him. She would reach out to him and set up a time to have coffee and conversation. She chose to be gentle in how she responded to him and spoke to him. She would not add to his pain. In other words, she chose to love Fred as Jesus loved him.

Reflecting on Anne's Story

Choosing to love Fred did not guarantee that Fred would ever change, but choosing to love Fred would change how Anne viewed him and related to him. It created the *possibility* for a different kind of relationship with him. Reacting to Fred out of her old issues and patterns guaranteed that nothing would change—not Fred, not Anne, not the relationship. Instead, choosing to love Fred through the power of the Spirit created the possibility for God to work—in Fred, in Anne, and in the relationship.

Whether or not Fred or the relationship ever changed, Anne's choice to love Fred allowed the Spirit to work in her life. It allowed the Spirit to bring some healing to the wounds associated with her old issues. It allowed the Spirit to move her beyond the control of her old fears. It allowed the Spirit to teach her new ways of thinking and responding. It allowed the Spirit to grow her spiritually. It allowed the spirit to fill her with the fruit of the Spirit in her relationship with Fred.

Anne's choice to love Fred also impacted her relationship with God. She learned to be more sensitive to the Spirit's nudges. She learned to follow where the Spirit led, trusting the Spirit's guidance. She learned to depend on the Spirit for the ability to do what she could not do in her own strength. She learned to live out of an attitude of prayer, sharing herself and her experiences with God. She learned to rest in her identity as a beloved child of God and as a committed follower of Jesus.

Anne's choice to love Fred, through the power of the Spirit, changed how she lived. It changed how she lived in relationship with others, especially those who pushed her buttons. It changed how she lived in relationship with God. It also taught her how to live out of joy and peace.

She learned how to be free from the power of the issues, hurts, fears, and patterns rooted in her past. Those issues, hurts, fears, and patterns did not magically disappear, but she learned how to deal with them in a way that set her free from their power over her life. When those issues, hurts, fears, and patterns resurfaced, she knew how to deal with them through the power of the Spirit. No longer would they keep her from loving as Jesus loved.

CHAPTER 11

Praying the Fruit of the Spirit

Paul's fruit of the Spirit can be used as a guide to prayer that fosters openness to the Spirit and the Spirit's work. When we combine breath prayer[35] with the fruit of the Spirit, we place ourselves in a position for the Spirit to work in us. Following the pattern of our breathing, we pray, "Fill me; cleanse me."

Fill me with your self-giving *love*.
> Cleanse me of my self-serving, what's-in-it-for-me, fear-based ego needs.

Fill me with your *joy*.
> Cleanse me of my frustration and anger, negativity and angst, depression and shame.

Fill me with your *peace*.
> Cleanse me of my anxiety and fear.

Fill me with your *patience*.
> Cleanse me of the expectations by which I judge others, which give birth to irritation and frustration when others do not measure up to those expectations.

Fill me with your *kindness.*

>Cleanse me of my critical, judgmental spirit.

Fill me with your *generosity.*

>Cleanse me of my inclination to withhold compassion, understanding, and forgiveness.

Fill me with your *faithfulness.*

>Cleanse me of how I hold myself emotionally aloof from others as though I am better than them and of how I emotionally distance myself from them.

Fill me with your *gentleness.*

>Cleanse me of harsh, demeaning thoughts, words, and actions.

Fill me with *self-control.*

>Cleanse me of my emotional reactive patterns that are the expression of my default, self-serving nature.

Praying the fruit of the Spirit puts us into a position for the Spirit to speak to us. As we pray each trait, the Spirit brings to mind individuals, relationships, and situations in which we react out of our default nature. This awareness is not intended to be a source of condemnation and guilt. Rather, it is the Spirit leading us into self-awareness so that we can practice self-control. The awareness becomes the Spirit's invitation to choose a different response. It becomes the Spirit's invitation to love as Jesus loved.

Fill me, Spirit of God, that I might love as Jesus loved!

POSTLUDE

Paul's description of the fruit of the Spirit reflects what the life of a follower of Jesus can look like through the transforming, empowering work of the Spirit.

The fruit of the Spirit teaches us that self-giving, servant love is the premier identifying mark of the follower of Jesus.

The fruit of the Spirit teaches us that love is expressed in grace-based relationships marked by patience, kindness and gentleness, and generosity and faithfulness. Paul's teaching about love in 1 Corinthians 13 teaches us that love moves us beyond a competitive spirit rooted in *better than, less than* thinking that divides the world into us and them categories.

The fruit of the Spirit teaches us that the ability to love as Jesus loved is inseparably tied to the inner spirit or disposition out of which we live. Joy and peace set us free to love as Jesus loved. Anxiety and fear, frustration and anger, and guilt and shame block the ability to love.

The fruit of the Spirit teaches us that the follower of Jesus lives with deep self-understanding. She understands her default nature that Paul called "the flesh." She recognizes the reality of the fear-based, self-focused, self-serving, what's-in-it-for-me spirit in her life. She understands how that spirit of fear manifests itself in her life. She understands the deceptive nature of her basic ego needs. This self-understanding leads her to gratefully claim God's gifts of grace and forgiveness. It leads her to gladly rely upon God's Spirit.

The fruit of the Spirit teaches us that the follower of Jesus lives with Spirit-directed self-awareness, making possible Spirit-empowered self-control. Thus, he consciously focuses on the inner spirit of his life lest he unconsciously revert to living out of his default nature and its fear-shaped patterns.

The fruit of the Spirit teaches us that the follower of Jesus lives in glad dependency upon the Spirit. Recognizing that he cannot in his own strength love as Jesus loved, he turns to the Spirit for the power to do what he cannot do alone. He consciously cultivates awareness of the Spirit and seeks to keep in step with the Spirit's guidance, direction, and work.

The fruit of the Spirit teaches us that the nine traits of the fruit of the Spirit mark out a path that, when followed, leads us to loving as Jesus loved. Through the work of the Spirit, we *can* love as Jesus loved.

In the fruit of the Spirit, the apostle Paul described the path that leads us to love as Jesus loved. May this explanation of these traits point you to that path. May the Spirit empower you to follow it!

SMALL GROUP STUDY GUIDE

Preface

- What thought in the preface captured your attention? Why?
- Read John 13:34–35. Jesus identified love as the distinguishing mark of his followers. What, other than love, do Christians today use to identify themselves? What reputations, other than love, do churches commonly have?
- What do you use to identify yourself as a follower of Jesus?
- What in your life operates as a barrier to loving as Jesus loved?

Chapter 1: The Fruit of the Spirit versus the Works of the Flesh

- What thought in chapter 1 captured your attention? Why?
- *The flesh* is described as the default spirit that is inherent to our human nature. What is your reaction

to the author's description of *the flesh*? What emotions does it stir? With which part of the description do you identify?

- What fear do you recognize behind the pattern of your life?

- Review the three categories of "the works of the flesh." Describe how *the flesh* produces "the works of the flesh." Which of the three categories do you recognize in your own life?

- The way we humans generally deal with *the flesh* and the works it produces is through laws—religious, moral, and legal codes that define right and wrong, good and bad. Identify some of the codes that have shaped your life through the years. What is the impact of those codes on your spiritual life?

- What is the downside of seeking to deal with *the flesh* through laws? Identify an example from your own experience.

- Rather than living in obedience to a code or law, Paul argued that the followers of Jesus live under the guidance of the Spirit. Living "by the Spirit" produces two things the Law cannot. The Spirit moves us beyond the spirit and patterns of *the flesh* and fills us with the fruit of the Spirit. Relate how you have experienced these two realities.

- Why is it difficult to believe that the Spirit can move us beyond our default nature and empower us to love as Jesus loved?

Chapter 2: The Path to Loving as Jesus Loved

- What thought in chapter 2 captured your attention? Why?
- Explore again the interdependent, interrelated nature of the nine traits identified as the fruit of the Spirit, identifying the three-piece structure the author identified within them. What does that structure communicate?
- Which of the nine traits is most difficult for you?

Chapter 3: Love, Joy, and Peace: The Spirit with Which We Live

- What thought in chapter 3 captured your attention? Why?
- The first three traits in the fruit of the Spirit deal with the spirit out of which we live. The next five deal with how we relate to others. What is the relationship between the spirit out of which we live and how we view and treat others? Share a personal experience that reflects this reality.
- Describe the interrelated nature of love, joy, and peace. How does your experience bear out this reality?
- Identify and share one way that the Spirit has transformed your heart and mind.

Chapter 4: The Fruit of the Spirit Is Love

- What thought in chapter 4 captured your attention? Why?
- Relate a time that you experienced self-giving, servant love from another.
- What makes it difficult to love "the least of these"?
- What makes our love selective?
- Love is expressed in how we relate to others. Which relational trait is most challenging for you: patience, kindness, generosity, faithfulness, or gentleness?
- Look again at what Paul said love "is not" in 1 Corinthians 13. Identify the "better than, less than" thinking underlying his descriptions. Relate an experience of what love "is not" and how it communicated "better than, less than" thinking.

Chapter 5: The Fruit of the Spirit Is Joy

- What thought in chapter 5 captured your attention? Why?
- Joy and peace set us free to love. What makes this statement true?
- With which example of emotional tone did you identify?
- Which of the four emotional-relational needs and their corresponding fears do you identify as your primary need and fear? What factors contributed to that need and fear being primary for you?

- What blocks the flow of joy in your life? What robs you of joy? What is the emotional tone of your life when joy is blocked?
- What practices do you follow that cultivate an awareness of God's goodness?

Chapter 6: The Fruit of the Spirit Is Peace

- What thought in chapter 6 captured your attention? Why?
- Review the distinction between anxiety and fear. Relate an experience of each.
- How does anxiety relate to the four emotional-relational needs and fears identified in chapter 5?
- The world's kind of peace is pursued by focusing on the threat "out there" and by seeking to control. What do these patterns look like in your life?
- Review the steps that were outlined in the path to peace. Which step presents the greatest challenge for you personally?
- Relate a time that you experienced the peace of God.

Chapter 7: The Fruit of the Spirit Is Grace-based Relationships

- What thought in chapter 7 captured your attention? Why?
- Review the five-part pattern that grows out of impatience. Reflect on a similar experience in your life, identifying each aspect of the pattern in your experience.

- The first aspect in this pattern is impatience. What is the relationship between impatience and expectations? What is the emotional tone associated with impatience? How does impatience blur our focus?
- How is the pattern that grows out of impatience an expression of earning, deserving, thinking, and relating?
- Compare each aspect of the impatience pattern with the five traits Paul listed: spatience, kindness, generosity, faithfulness, and gentleness. How are these five traits expressions of grace and the face of love?
- What did you learn about yourself from this chapter?

Chapter 8: The Fruit of the Spirit Is Self-Control

- What thought in chapter 8 captured your attention? Why?
- What factors make it difficult to believe that we can love as Jesus loved?
- What, other than loving as Jesus loved, do you use to identify yourself as a follower of Jesus?
- Self-control is identified as the key trait to the other eight traits identified in the fruit of the Spirit. As such, it is the key to loving as Jesus loved. Explain why this trait is foundational to the other eight.
- Relate your knowledge of and experience with breath prayer. How does it relate to self-control?

Chapter 9: Keep in Step with the Spirit

- What thought in chapter 9 captured your attention? Why?
- What does the phrase "dance to the rhythm of God's love and forgiveness" communicate to you?
- What factors make it difficult to allow the Spirit to lead or to follow the Spirit's lead?
- What is involved in learning to keep in step with the Spirit? What practices help you do so?
- What does the author say is the result of following the Spirit's lead? Of not following the Spirit's lead? How does your experience bear out his thought?

Chapter 10: Anne's Story

- What thought in chapter 10 captured your attention? Why?
- With which part of Anne's story did you identify? Why?
- What emotion did Anne's story stir in you?
- Reflect on a difficult relationship. Identify the nature of the relationship. Visualize how the path that has been described might impact that relationship.

Chapter 11: Praying the Fruit of the Spirit

- What thought in Chapter 11 captured your attention? Why?
- Practice praying the fruit of the Spirit, paying attention to what the Spirit brings to your awareness. Journal your experience.

Postlude

- What thought in the postlude captured your attention? Why?
- What is your reaction to the author's description of what it means to live as a follower of Jesus? How is that description in line with or at odds with your own understanding of what it means to live as a follower of Jesus?
- How has this study impacted your life?
- What is your key takeaway?
- What is your next step?

About the Author

Steve Langford, also known as Pastor Steve, has given his adult life to the study and teaching of scripture in the local church. Within the religious communities in which he has walked and in the churches he has served, he is known as a gifted teacher and an insightful spiritual guide who does not shrink from prophetically proclaiming the truth of scripture. His teaching focuses on the original message of the biblical text as a foundation for knowing God and as a resource for the transformation of heart and mind called spiritual formation. Pastor Steve is a lifelong student, having earned degrees in biblical studies from Howard Payne University in Brownwood, Texas, and from Southwestern Baptist Theological Seminary in Fort Worth, Texas, (MDiv, 1973; DMin, 1993). His postgraduate studies have been in Bowen Family Systems theory with an emphasis upon leadership rooted in self-awareness and self-management.

Dr. Langford and Etta, his wife of forty-nine years, have three adult sons—Josh, Jon, and Justin—and four grandchildren: Damon, Lillian, Scarlett, and Axel.

ENDNOTES

1   Such love is expressed in using one's power, in its varied forms, for the benefit of another—often at great cost to one's self.

2   All scripture quotations are from the New Revised Standard Version, unless otherwise indicated, copyright © 1989 the Division of Christian Education of the National Council of the Churches of Christ in the United States of America. Used by permission.

3   In contrast to the fruit (singular) of the Spirit, the works (plural) of the flesh are manifold.

4   The law appeals to the human ego. Keeping the law is dependent on self-effort. Thus, to keep the law translates into the subtle message that I am adequate and, therefore, okay. Keeping the law also allows us to distance ourselves from those who don't keep the law, viewing them as *less than* or inadequate (us-them polarization). Thus, it fosters an unconscious sense of superiority and spiritual arrogance.

5   See Galatians 1:6–9; 3:1–5; 5:7–8.

6   Compare Romans 8:2–8.

7   John 14:25–26 and 16:12–15 speak of the Spirit's work of teaching the ways of God that Jesus taught.

8   Genesis 1:26.

9   1 John 4:7–8.

10 Jesus identified love as the distinguishing mark of his followers in John 13:35: "By this everyone will know that you are my disciples, if you have love for one another." Self-giving, servant love—not religious belief or church involvement or moral behavior or a stand on particular moral issue—is what identifies us as followers of Jesus.

11 Jesus's emphasis on the powerless and poor reflects the teachings of the Hebrew prophets. See Isaiah 1:17 and Jeremiah 7:5–7 as examples.

12 This fear often surfaces as anger when we feel discounted or devalued.

13 Generally, one of the four becomes dominant, overshadowing the other three.

14 Matthew 7:3–5.

15 God's *goodness* refers to those dimensions of life that are pure gift. They are given by God to all, independent of our work or our deserving. They are given freely, generously, and abundantly to enrich our lives. God's goodness includes the beauty of creation in all its diversity and splendor, the capacity for physical pleasure through the physical senses that allow us to experience God's creation, the ability to learn and discover, to develop and grow, the pleasure of creativity and accomplishment, the ability to share life deeply and meaningfully in close relationship, the pleasure of two celebrating their connectedness through the gift of sexuality. All are simple pleasures, a part of life's goodness. They are gifts of God's creation that anyone can experience. The Spirit calls us to slow down, to pay attention, and to recognize and accept these gifts of God's goodness. When we are aware of these gifts, a spirit of wonder, gratitude, and abundance grows within us. Joy flows out of recognizing and opening oneself to the goodness of God and to the gift-nature of life. The goodness of God is an expression of God's *grace*. But grace also has a more personal, individual touch. Grace is our experience of being accepted unconditionally, forgiven freely, and embraced joyfully as beloved child. Whereas God's goodness is not related to what we deserve, God's grace is the opposite of what we deserve. It is what we receive from God as we face and deal with the weaknesses, limitations, and failures that are a part of being human. Joy is birthed within as we experience the cleansing touch of God's forgiveness. A spirit of thanksgiving and praise grows within us as we experience grace that frees us from condemnation, judgment, guilt, and shame. As we learn to claim God's grace and rest in God's love, joy flows from the heart. God's *faithfulness* speaks of God's unfailing commitment to us. It speaks of God's walking in relationship with us, bringing us to healing and wholeness, to growth and maturity. It proclaims that God never gives up on us or abandons us. We experience God's faithfulness in all of life, particularly in the midst of life's painful, wounding events. As we walk difficult paths, through painful times, God is faithful to us. God strengthens and sustains us in the midst of the event. God uses the experience to teach and mature us as well as deepen and enrich our lives. God transforms what the difficult, painful times do to us, bringing good out of evil, gain out of loss, and progress out of pain. As we experience God's sustaining grace in the midst of life's difficulties, joy is birthed within. As we experience the good that God brings out of those

difficult times—the healing, the growth, the depth, and the richness of life—a spirit of thanksgiving wells up inside us, feeding the joy growing in the heart. As we become secure in God's faithfulness and confident in how God will transform any event, joy flows from the heart. We experience joy as the Spirit leads us to recognize and open ourselves to the goodness of God, the grace of God, and the faithfulness of God.

16 Nehemiah 8:10.

17 While we have no control over what happens in life, we do have control over how we respond to what happens. Our response to an event has a greater impact on us than the event itself.

18 We call this kind of mental-emotional fixation *worry*. Such worry is an attempt to find a way to take control of something over which we have no control. It is evidence that we are under the control of our fear.

19 Managing one's fear is reflected in Reinhold Niebuhr's Serenity Prayer, which is central to the recovery movement: "God, grant me the serenity (peace) to accept the things I cannot change, courage to change the things I can, and the wisdom to know the difference." To "accept the things I cannot change" is to trust into God's care and work those things over which I have no power or control. "The courage to change the things I can" is to focus on the only thing over which I have any control, that is, myself—my thinking, my feelings, my reactions, and my actions. "The wisdom to know the difference" is to recognize boundaries. Boundaries define what is mine and what isn't, what I am responsible for and what I am not, and what I have control over and what I do not. Such wisdom is God's gift to us through the Spirit. From childhood, we have been taught to focus on others and attempt to control what they do or think. Wisdom leads us beyond this "out there" focus to recognize and choose to manage ourselves.

20 The journey into peace follows the path of prayer. This truth is reflected in Jesus's experience of prayer in the Garden of Gethsemane (Mark 14:32–42). Jesus entered the garden distressed and in turmoil. He shared his struggle with God in prayer, expressing his desire to escape what lay ahead along with his desire to do God's will. He continued to pray until he found peace. That peace was reflected in the strength with which he dealt with Judas and the crowd that came to arrest him. That peace continued to sustain him, first as he stood trial before the hostile Jewish Sanhedrin and then when he went before the Roman governor Pilate.

21 The phrase "earning-deserving" describes a way of living in relationship with others that is based on how the other measures up to a prescribed standard or set of expectations. The other is treated in a way they "deserve" based on

how they conformed or failed to conform to the standard. Earning-deserving is another way of talking about merit and reward. Relating out of earning-deserving thinking is the opposite of grace.

22   That pain always involves, but is not limited to, the pain of condemnation and rejection that plays on our inherent need to be valued and accepted.

23   LGBTQ refers to issues related to sexual orientation. It is an abbreviation for lesbian, gay, bisexual, transgender, and queer.

24   Most religious groups identify themselves in terms of right belief, right ritual, and right behavior (morals).

25   When we continue to live in and with our inner turmoil, our thinking fuels that inner turmoil. We become trapped in an unending spiral in which our thinking fuels our feelings of anxiety, fear, frustration, and anger—and our feelings of anxiety, fear, frustration, and anger fuel our thinking. We become our own worst enemies, keeping ourselves trapped in our feelings of anxiety, fear, frustration, and anger.

26   For examples of these patterns, see the discussion about emotional tone in chapter 5.

27   See again "The Journey into Peace" in chapter 6.

28   The Holy Bible, New International Version®, NIV® Copyright © 1973, 1978, 1984, 2011 by Biblica, Inc.™ Used by permission. All rights reserved worldwide.

29   See again chapter 8.

30   This awareness is inseparably tied to self-knowledge and self-awareness. See again chapter 8.

31   The term *confident humility* expresses the idea of being confident in the gifts and abilities that God has given me without feeling superior or better than others because of those gifts. The confidence is tempered by humility, the deep knowledge that all of my abilities are gifts from God. Confident humility frees us to offer our gifts and abilities out of a spirit of joyous generosity as the Spirit leads us.

32   See Jesus's teachings in Mark 8:34–37 and parallel texts.

33   This emphasis upon belief and morals often becomes a new form of law after which we pattern our lives and judge others.

34   Anne and Fred are fictional characters. Their stories are a composite of multiple real-life experiences.

35   Breath prayer is described in chapter 8.

CPSIA information can be obtained
at www.ICGtesting.com
Printed in the USA
BVHW071105271221
624762BV00001B/58

9 781973 652946